KS1
Success
Workbook

Lynn Huggins-Cooper

Science

Contents

Plants and animals

Humans

Materials

Physical processes

Test practice

Answers

See additional answer booklet

Parts of a plant

Precious parts

Write down the correct parts of this plant using the words in the box.

leaf

stem

root

flower

1 _____ _____

2 _____ _____

3 _____ _____

4 _____ _____

Hard at work

Match the parts of the plant to the job they do.

a Makes food for the plant.

b Holds the plant in the soil.

c Carries water and goodness around the plant.

d Attracts insects.

1 _____

2 _____

3 _____

4 _____

Flowers are my favourite part, because they're so pretty.

I like the roots best, because they include yummy carrots!

Picture this

Draw the part of the plant described under each box.

1 Holds the plant in the soil.

2 Makes food for the plant.

3 Attracts insects.

4 Carries water and goodness around the plant.

The complete plant

Draw a picture of a plant in this box. Then add the labels yourself!

Top Tip *When you have vegetables at home, try to work out which part of a plant they are – cabbage is the leaves of a cabbage plant, carrots are a root vegetable, etc.*

Senses

Famous five

What are our five senses? Write them here.

1 _____

2 _____

3 _____

4 _____

5 _____

Which part?

Draw a line to match the sense to the correct part of the body.

1 hearing   **2** seeing   **3** feeling   **4** tasting   **5** smelling

A part to play

Label this picture with the correct senses. Use the words in the box to help you.

| seeing | feeling | tasting | smelling | hearing |

1 [_____]

2 [_____]

3 [_____]

4 [_____]

5 [_____]

Sensible choice!

1   Which sense do you use when you sniff a flower?   _____

2   Which sense do you use when you enjoy a
    cream cake?   _____

3   Which sense do you use when you stroke a soft cat?   _____

4   Which sense do you use when you listen to music?   _____

5   Which sense do you use when you look at a sunset?   _____

Top Tip *Keep a senses diary through the day. It will help you to realise how much our senses tell us about the world!*

Pooh! What's that smell?

If you had any sense, you'd know...!

Reuse and recycle

Litter facts

Write down the answers to these questions.

1 What is litter? _____

_____

2 What is recycling? _____

_____

_____

3 What sort of objects and materials can be easily recycled?

_____

_____

4 What sort of objects could be reused instead of thrown away?

_____

_____

Danger!

Rubbish and litter can be dangerous to animals. Draw a line to match the two parts of each sentence to say what can happen.

1 Hedgehogs can get tangled

2 Swans can be poisoned

3 Seals can choke

4 Sea birds can get caught

a ...in the plastic rings that keep cans together in packs.

b ...in fishing line left on the beach.

c ...when they eat lead fishing weights and lures.

d ...when they eat plastic bags floating in the water – they look like jellyfish.

Reuse or recycle?

Look at this list of things. Draw the items that can be recycled in the box.

1 plastic carrier bag

2 cardboard egg box

3 newspaper

4 glass bottle

5 plastic milk bottle

6 drinks can

7 dog food can

8 clear plastic food bag

9 magazine

10 squash bottle

Make sure you take reusable bags when you go to the supermarket – it is good for the environment, and it saves money, too! You could make your own bag from cloth.

Don't drop litter!

Draw a poster that tells people not to drop litter. Remember to explain why this is important.

Your room is a tip!

That's utter rubbish!

Living things

Is it alive?

Write down the seven things that tell us something is alive.

1 _____

2 _____

3 _____

4 _____

5 _____

6 _____

7 _____

Top Tip *It is difficult to see all seven things happening in a plant. They do not walk about, but they do move! They grow towards the light, for example.*

Alive or not alive?

Draw a circle round the things that are alive.

Alive or once alive?

Alive or once alive? Draw a circle round the things that were alive once, but not now.

Is it alive?

Draw four things that are alive in the butterfly shape.

Sam's alive – he eats enough!

And you don't?

Sorting

Sorting animals and plants

Help to sort these things into groups by writing 'animal' or 'plant' under each of them.

1
_____

2
_____

3
_____

4
_____

5
_____

6
_____

7
_____

8
_____

Sorting bugs and birds

Bug or bird? Draw the bugs in the box labelled bugs and the birds in the box labelled birds.

bugs	**birds**

When you are sorting anything, look for what is the same and what is different about the things you are sorting. It will help you to put them into groups.

Sorting fur and feathers

Fur or feathers? Write fur or feathers under each picture.

1

2

3

4

_____ _____ _____ _____

5

6

7

8

_____ _____ _____ _____

Your turn

List the ways you could sort these animals into two groups.

butterfly ladybird spider dragonfly blackbird cat horse rabbit

An example has been done for you.

Things that fly/Things that do not fly _____

_____

_____

Sherbet and chocolate could be in the same set, because they're both types of sweet.

Or they could be in the same set, because I've just eaten them both...

Plant investigation

The parts of a plant

Have a look at a plant in your garden or the park. See if you can name all of the different parts.

Ask permission from an adult and dig up a dandelion. Rinse the roots and look at the plant carefully. Can you see all of the parts below?

Write the job each part does on the labels.

Plant diagram

Draw your plant here. Don't forget the labels!

I'm off to give a dandelion to my rabbit!

He'll love the roots – after all he's always eating carrots!

Senses investigation

Touch

Feel and explore surfaces and textures with your fingers. Then write the words you can think of to describe them here.

_____

_____

_____

_____

Smell

Write words to describe the smells you discover.

_____

_____

_____

_____

_____

I love using my senses to explore the world!

Poo! I just 'explored' the shoe rack and your trainers are whiffy!

Taste

How many different tastes can you find?
Describe your tastes here.

_____

_____

_____

_____

Top Tip *Always be careful when you taste something. Check with an adult that it is safe to eat.*

Hear

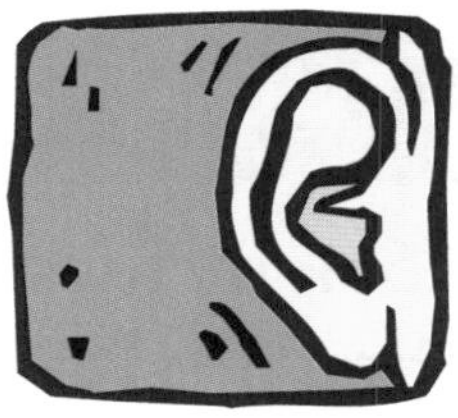

What different sounds can you hear?
Describe them here.

_____

_____

_____

_____

See

What are the most interesting things you can see?
Describe them here.

_____

_____

_____

_____

Healthy eating

Which is healthier?

Tick the healthier meal from each pair.

1   Fried egg and chips ☐ OR egg salad sandwich? ☐

2   Baked potato and cottage cheese salad ☐ OR fish and chips? ☐

3   Fried breakfast ☐ OR pasta with tomato sauce? ☐

4   Scrambled egg on wholemeal toast ☐ OR takeaway pizza? ☐

5   Tuna salad with boiled new potatoes ☐ OR pie and mash? ☐

True or false?

Look at these sentences. Write 'T' in the box if they are true and 'F' if they are false.

1   We do not need to eat lots of fruit and vegetables. ☐

2   We need plenty of sleep. ☐

3   Sugary drinks are good for you, so drink lots. ☐

4   We should eat as many sweets as we can every day to exercise our teeth. ☐

5   We should take exercise, including running about and playing games, to keep healthy. ☐

6   We should eat fresh fruit and vegetables every day. ☐

Top Tip

Remember – no food is 'bad', but you need to eat a balanced diet with lots of different foods to stay healthy.

Lovely lunches

Look back at the tasks you have done on healthy eating. Use what you have learnt to draw a healthy lunch here.

What is their job?

Draw a line to match the foods to the jobs they do.

pasta

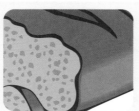

cereals and bread

cheese, nuts and milk

fruit and vegetables

1 Give us vitamins and fibre

2 Help us to grow and heal when we are hurt

3 Give us fibre, which helps us to digest our food

4 Gives us energy to run and play

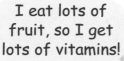

I eat lots of fruit, so I get lots of vitamins!

If you ate lots of sticky jaw toffee, I'd get lots of peace...

Bones and muscles

Find those bones!

Write the correct labels on the skeleton. Use the words in the box to help you.

backbone (spine)

skull

ribs

pelvis

kneecap

1 [   ]

2 [   ]

3 [   ]

4 [   ]

5 [   ]

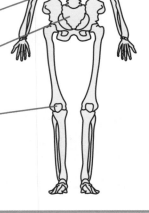

Name their job

Write down the answers to these questions.

1   Why do we need bones?

_____

2   What does our skull protect?

_____

3   What are the bones called that protect our soft insides, like our lungs?

_____

4   What is the bone called that runs in a line up our back?

_____

5   Why do we need muscles?

_____

Bones and muscles

Complete each sentence by writing the correct word from the box.

floppy   tighten   move   bones   muscles   protect

If we did not have _____, we would be all _____!
Bones help us to stand up and _____. They _____
the soft parts of our body, like our brain. _____ help our
bones to move. When I bend my arm, the muscles _____ up
and help to pull the bones where I want them to go.

Top Tip *If you bend your knee, you can feel the muscles and bones moving!*

True or false?

Tick the statements that are true.

1   The name of the bone that protects the brain is the skull. ☐

2   Our kneecaps are the bones that protect our heart and lungs. ☐

3   Bones support my body. Without them, I would be all stiff! ☐

4   Bones and muscles work together to help me move. ☐

5   There are no bones in my arms. ☐

6   Bones support my body. Without them, I would be all floppy! ☐

Look! I'm a wobbly jelly – I have no bones!

Are you sure it's not your brain that's missing?

Teeth

What is their job?

Write down the job each type of tooth does.

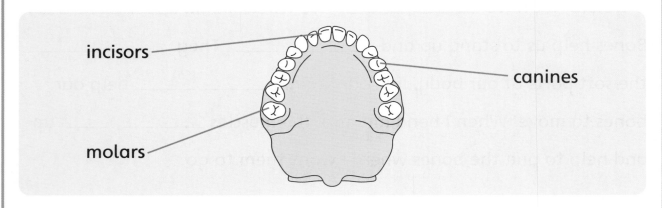

incisors

canines

molars

1   The pointed teeth are called canines.

They are for _____.

2   The teeth at the front are called incisors.

They are for _____.

3   The teeth at the back are called molars.

They are for _____.

Top Tip

Wash your hands, then feel your teeth. Now try to find the molars, incisors and canines in your mouth!

Which is which?

Draw the correct tooth in the boxes to match each type of tooth.

1 incisor	2 canine	3 molar

Healthy habits

What should you do to keep your teeth healthy? Tick the correct answers.

1   Eat lots of sweets. ☐

2   Drink lots of sugary drinks. ☐

3   Visit the dentist twice a year for check-ups. ☐

4   Clean your teeth twice a day. ☐

5   Eat raw vegetables. ☐

6   Do not drink too many sugary drinks. ☐

True or false?

Look at these sentences. Write 'T' in the box if they are true and 'F' if they are false.

1   Eating lots of sweets is good for your teeth. ☐

2   You should never brush your teeth, because you might hurt them. ☐

3   The big teeth at the front of your mouth are called molars. ☐

4   Guinea pigs have long front teeth called incisors. ☐

5   Canines are used for grinding food. ☐

I like going to the dentist – I get a sticker!

I like going HOME from the dentist!

Healthy eating investigation

A healthy meal

You are going to plan and make a healthy sandwich. You can find out lots of information about healthy eating on the Internet. Look at this site to find out about healthy bread.

http://www.warburtons.co.uk/

Bread is good for you!

Write what you found out about healthy bread here:

Cyber sandwiches

You can also have fun on this website, creating cyber sandwiches! This will give you ideas about what to put in your own sandwich.

http://www.unilever.com/ourvalues/nutritionhygienepersonalcare/nutrition/Nutritionalfun/fat/sandwichtools/

A balanced meal

Remember, a healthy meal is balanced. That means you need a variety of different types of food.

Protein food to help us to grow and repair, such as cheese and eggs.

Fibre and vitamin-filled fruit and vegetables.

Energy food such as bread and pasta.

Fats such as olive oil and butter.

Write a description of the sandwich you are going to make. Explain why you have chosen the different ingredients. Then go and make the sandwich!

_____

_____

_____

_____

_____

Cheese and tomato is my favourite!

I like peanut butter – I pretend it's a mud sandwich – yum!

Body investigation

Make a skeleton that moves!

You will need these things:

Tracing or baking paper (or even thin printer paper)

Pencil

Card

Paper clips

Scissors

Split pins (which you can get from a newsagents or stationers)

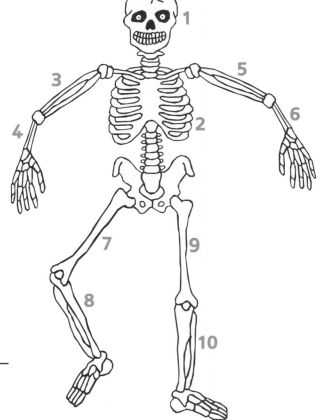

1   Using the tracing paper and pencil, trace the parts of the skeleton on page 27.

2   Use a paper clip to attach the tracing paper to a piece of card – packaging is fine.

3   Cut out the pieces of card. Then join them together with split pins.

4   Make your skeleton move! Bend your arm at the elbow, then bend your skeleton's arm. You could echo the movements you make to explain to somebody how your skeleton works!

I'm off to frighten mum with my skeleton model!

She'll rattle your bones if you do!

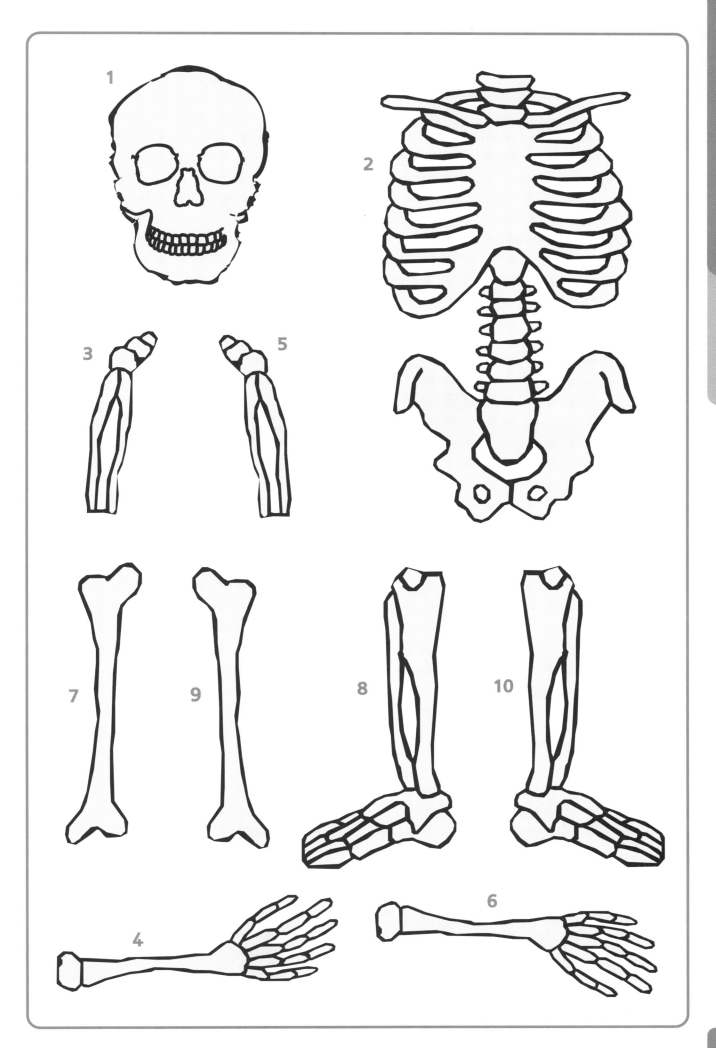

Floating and sinking

Will it float?

Which things shown here will float?

Draw the things you choose in the boat shape below.

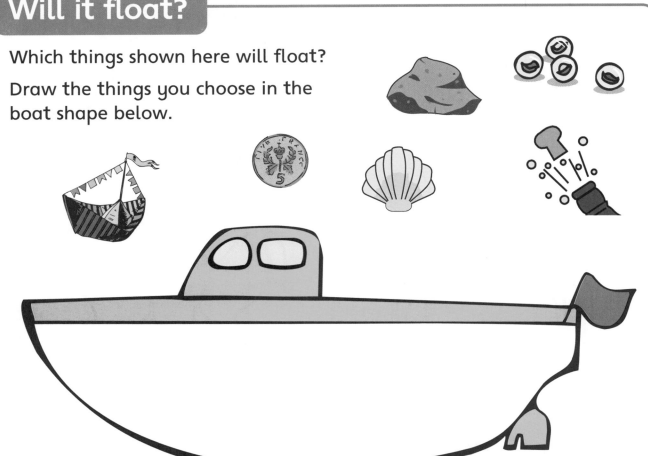

Sink or float?

Draw a line to match the first half of each sentence to the second half, so they make sense.

1	Some things float	a	...heavy for its size.
2	A pebble would	b	...light for their size.
3	Things float when they are	c	...but a nail would sink.
4	A stone sinks because it is	d	...and others sink.
5	A matchstick would float	e	...sink, but a plastic cup would float.

Letts

KS1 Success

Workbook Answer Booklet

Science

Answers

Plants and animals

PAGES 4–5 PARTS OF A PLANT

Precious parts

1	flower	3	stem
2	leaf	4	root

Hard at work

1	d	3	c
2	a	4	b

Picture this

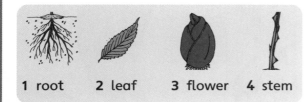

1 root   2 leaf   3 flower   4 stem

The complete plant

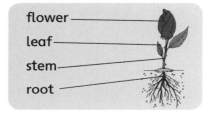

flower
leaf
stem
root

PAGES 6–7 SENSES

Famous five

in any order: seeing, hearing, feeling, tasting, smelling

Which part?

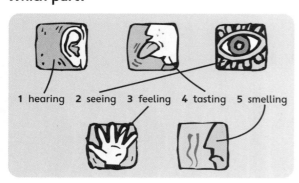

1 hearing   2 seeing   3 feeling   4 tasting   5 smelling

A part to play

1	seeing	4	hearing
2	smelling	5	tasting
3	feeling		

Sensible choice!

1	smelling	4	hearing
2	tasting	5	seeing
3	feeling		

PAGES 8–9 REUSE AND RECYCLE

Litter facts

1   Litter is rubbish left lying round.

2   Recycling is taking glass, paper, cans and sometimes plastic to be re-made into other useful objects.

3   paper, glass, cans

4   a variety of answers such as: carrier bags, yoghurt pots to grow seeds; plastic bottles cut in half and the top turned upside down as a funnel, etc.

Danger!

1	→ a	3	→ d
2	→ c	4	→ b

Reuse or recycle?

2, 3, 4, 5, 6, 7, 9 and 10 should be drawn in the box

Don't drop litter!

poster containing information about the dangers of litter

PAGES 10–11 LIVING THINGS

Is it alive?

It breathes.
It gets rid of waste.
It has babies.
It feeds.
It moves.
It feels things.
It grows and changes.

Alive or not alive?

Alive or once alive?

Is it alive?

a variety of answers such as:
cat, mouse, moth, grass

PAGES 12–13 SORTING

Sorting animals and plants

1	animal	5	animal
2	plant	6	animal
3	animal	7	plant
4	plant	8	plant

Sorting bugs and birds

bugs: snail, ladybird, beetle, worm

birds: penguin, owl, swan, hen

Sorting fur and feathers

1	fur	5	fur
2	feathers	6	fur
3	feathers	7	feathers
4	fur	8	feathers

Your turn

a variety of answers such as: bugs/not bugs, eats plants/eats other creatures, has 4 legs/has more than 4 legs

Humans

PAGES 18–19 HEALTHY EATING

Which is healthier?

ticked options are:

1 egg salad sandwich

2 baked potato and cottage cheese salad

3 pasta with tomato sauce

4 scrambled egg on wholemeal toast

5 tuna salad with boiled new potatoes

True or false?

1	F	4	F
2	T	5	T
3	F	6	T

Lovely lunches

any healthy balanced meal

What is their job?

1 → fruit and vegetables

2 → cheese, nuts and milk

3 → cereals and bread

4 → pasta

PAGES 20–21 BONES AND MUSCLES

Find those bones!

1	skull	4	pelvis
2	ribs	5	kneecap
3	backbone (spine)		

Name their job

1 to support our bodies; to help us to move; to protect soft bits like our brain and heart

2 our brain

3 ribs

4 backbone or spine

5 because they work with our bones to help us to move

Bones and muscles

If we did not have **bones**, we would be all **floppy**! Bones help us to stand up and **move**. They **protect** the soft parts of our body, like our brain. **Muscles** help our bones to move. When I bend my arm, the muscles **tighten** up and help to pull the bones where I want them to go.

True or false?
ticked statements are: 1, 4 and 6

PAGES 22–23 TEETH
What is their job?
1 tearing
2 cutting and biting
3 chewing and grinding

Which is which?

1 incisor   2 canine   3 molar

Healthy habits
ticked answers are: 3, 4, 5 and 6

True or false?
1 F   4 T
2 F   5 F
3 F

Materials

PAGES 28–29 FLOATING AND SINKING
Will it float?
drawn items are:

Sink or float?
1 → d   4 → a
2 → e   5 → c
3 → b

Will it sink?
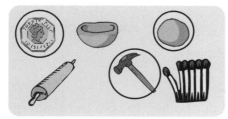

Make it float!
explanation that by flattening the Plasticine™ the water then pushes up on the bottom of it; making a big surface has made the Plasticine™ light for its size, etc.

PAGES 30–31 IS IT NATURAL?
Nature's own

People power
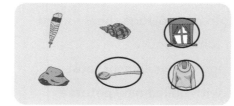

Where does it come from?

Sorting materials

a variety of answers such as: natural things – feathers, stones and shells; made by people – plastic bottle, polystyrene cup and a knife

PAGES 32–33 FINDING OUT ABOUT MATERIALS

Soft or hard?

Teddy: bunny, pillow, hat, bobble

Rock: car, spoon, book

Smooth or rough?

1 rough
2 smooth
3 rough
4 smooth
5 smooth

Can you see through it?

What is it made from?

1 → lunchbox
2 → teddy
3 → door
4 → skirt
5 → wall

PAGES 34–35 SOLID, LIQUID OR GAS?

What state is it?

1 S
2 S
3 G
4 G
5 L
6 L

Solid, liquid or gas?

1 G
2 S
3 L
4 S
5 G

Reversible changes

Irreversible changes

ticked answers are: 2, 3 and 4

Physical processes

PAGES 40–41 ELECTRICITY

Which ones use electricity?

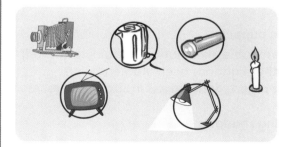

Battery or mains?

ticked items are:
2 Hi-fi
4 TV
7 CD player

Sound sources

Match it up

1 → c
2 → a
3 → b
4 → e
5 → d

PAGES 42–43 SOUND

Sounds good!

ticked sentences are: 1, 3 and 5

Safe sounds

a variety of answers such as:

1 You could damage your ears and your hearing.

2 a variety of answers such as: cars, sirens, alarms, buses, etc.

3 a variety of answers such as: sirens, machinery, motors, explosions, etc.

4 a variety of answers such as: mouse, pin dropping, bird singing, snow falling, etc.

5 to avoid ear damage

Hear, hear

Loud or quiet?

a variety of answers. Ask the child to make a list of quiet and loud noises.

PAGES 44–45 FORCES

Push or pull?

1	push	4	pull
2	push	5	push
3	push		

Gravity

1	force	4	float
2	fall	5	Moon
3	pulled	6	smaller

Friction

1	dry tiles	4	a dry playground
2	dry path	5	dry hands
3	a hill with no snow	6	wet hands

Which force?

1 friction

2 gravity

3 because of less friction – water coats the floor and makes it slippery

4 friction

5 a rough surface

PAGES 46–47 SOURCES OF LIGHT

Things that give off light

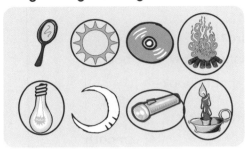

Lovely light

ticked sentences are: 1, 3, 4, 5 and 7

Let it glow!

Can you see it?

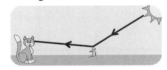

PAGES 48–49 SHADOWS

Shadows

1 → e		4 → d	
2 → b		5 → c	
3 → a			

Shadow puppets

any reasonable explanation containing the key points that light has been blocked by an opaque object; light travels in straight lines, etc.

Changing shadows

1 → b	2 → a

Where is the Sun?

sunset   midday   sunrise

Test practice

PAGES 52–56 TEST PRACTICE

1 a b c

2

hearing   seeing   touching

tasting   smelling

3 a variety of answers such as: glass bottle, jam jar, cat food tin, bean tin, drinks can, newspaper, comic, magazine, etc.

4 a variety of answers as long as they are plants and animals

5 Can fly: robin, butterfly

Cannot fly: dog, penguin, horse, crab

6 ticked items are:

  a apples   **c** cubes of cheese

  b orange juice **d** milk

7 1 → b

  2 → c

  3 → a

8 **a** molars

  b canines

  c incisors

9 a variety of answers such as: shell, pebble, feather, etc.

10 a variety of answers such as: pebble, stone, metal spoon, marble, metal toy car, shell

11 1 → e   4 → b

   2 → a   5 → c

   3 → d

12 a S   e L

    b L   f S

    c S   g G

    d G   h L

13 ticked answer is: d

14 ticked items are: b, d, e, g, h, i, j and n

15 a variety of answers such as: electrically operated toys, torch, portable radios and CD players, TV remote control

16

17 **a** gravity

  b friction

18 The light hits the butterfly, bounces off and enters the girl's eye.

19 a   b

Published by Letts Educational
An imprint of HarperCollins*Publishers*
77–85 Fulham Palace Road
London W6 8JB

Telephone: 0844 576 8126
Fax: 0844 576 8131
Email: education@harpercollins.co.uk

9781843157458

12

First published 2007

Text © Lynn Huggins-Cooper

Design and illustration © 2006 Letts Educational

Author: Lynn Huggins-Cooper
Book concept and development: Helen Jacobs
Project editor: Lily Morgan
Editorial and design: 2ibooks [publishing solutions] Cambridge
Illustrator: Piers Baker
Cover design: Angela English

Every effort has been made to trace copyright holders and obtain their permission for the use of copyright material. The authors and publishers will gladly receive information enabling them to rectify any error or omission in subsequent editions.

All facts are correct at time of going to press.

British Library Cataloging in Publication Data.

A CIP record of this book is available from the British Library.

MIX
Paper from
responsible sources
FSC® C007454

FSC™ is a non-profit international organisation established to promote the responsible management of the world's forests. Products carrying the FSC label are independently certified to assure consumers that they come from forests that are managed to meet the social, economic and ecological needs of present and future generations, and other controlled sources.

Find out more about HarperCollins and the environment at
www.harpercollins.co.uk/green

Will it sink?

Draw a circle round the things that will sink.

Make it float!

How could you make a ball of Plasticine™ float? Why would your idea work?

_____

_____

_____

_____

_____

_____

_____   *Find out about how boats float. Now try to find out something about the Plimsoll line!*

_____

Top Tip

I love floating in the sea.

I love pretending to be a shark!

Is it natural?

Nature's own

Draw a circle round the natural things.

How many natural materials can you find in your house? Make a list.

People power

Draw a circle round the materials that have been made by people.

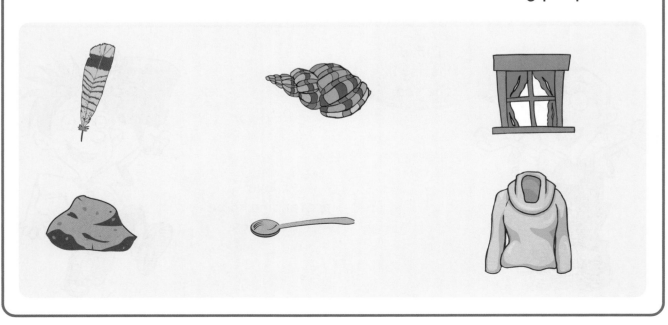

Where does it come from?

Draw a line to match the material to where it came from. For example, a pillow can be filled with feathers, so the pillow is joined to the feather. Now try the rest!

Sorting materials

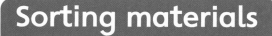

Draw three natural things in the leaf outline. Then draw three things made by people in the bag outline.

I like my leather jacket – naturally, I look cool in it!

Not!

Finding out about materials

Soft or hard?

Look at these things. Draw the soft ones in the teddy shape. Then draw the hard ones in the rock shape.

Smooth or rough?

Smooth or rough? Write 'rough' underneath the pictures of rough objects and 'smooth' under the pictures of smooth objects.

1 _____ 2 _____ 3 _____ 4 _____ 5 _____

Can you see through it?

Draw a circle round materials that are transparent (see-through).

What is it made from?

Draw a line from the material to the object you can make from it.

1 plastic   **2** fur fabric   **3** wood   **4** fabric   **5** stone

teddy   door   wall   lunchbox   skirt

My favourite teddy is made out of soft fur fabric.

My favourite toy is a hard plastic crocodile!

Solid, liquid or gas?

What state is it?

Are the things circled in purple solid, liquid or gas. Write 'S', 'L' or 'G' in the boxes.

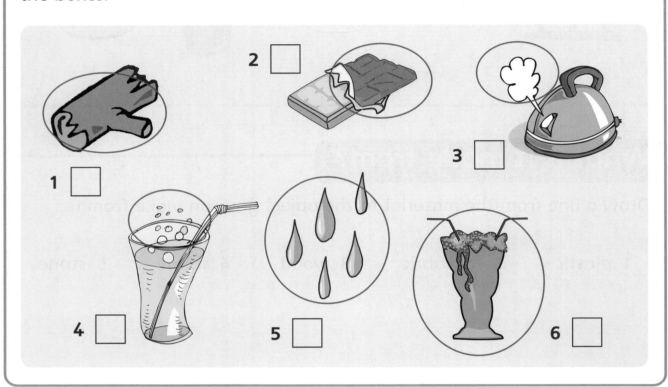

Solid, liquid or gas?

Are the things circled in blue solid, liquid or gas? Write 'S', 'L' or 'G' in the boxes.

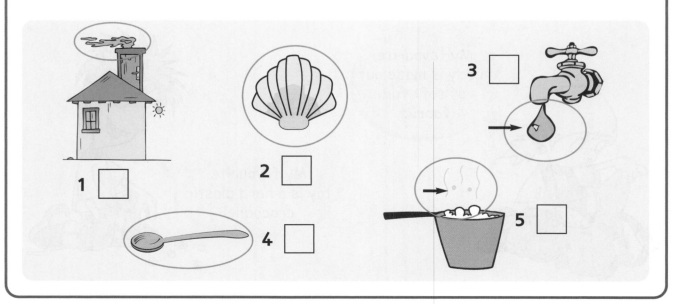

Reversible changes

Draw a circle round the changes that are reversible (the things which can be changed and changed back to their original state).

Irreversible changes

Tick the box that describes changes that are irreversible (the things which cannot change back to their original state).

1   steam coming from pan ☐

2   paper burning ☐

3   cake being baked ☐

4   pancake being fried ☐

5   ice freezing ☐

 **Top Tip** *Next time you eat a cake – or make one – think about how the ingredients have changed. Make a list of any that can be changed back.*

I'm going to make some ice cubes for a drink.

Just make sure they don't melt everywhere, or you'll see mum change state!

Float or sink investigation

What will float?

Make a collection of these things from around the house and garden:

Paper clip

Yoghurt pot

Marble

Plastic pen

Pebble

Leaf

Twig

Feather

Metal spoon

Plastic spoon

Crumpled ball of paper

Plastic block from construction kit

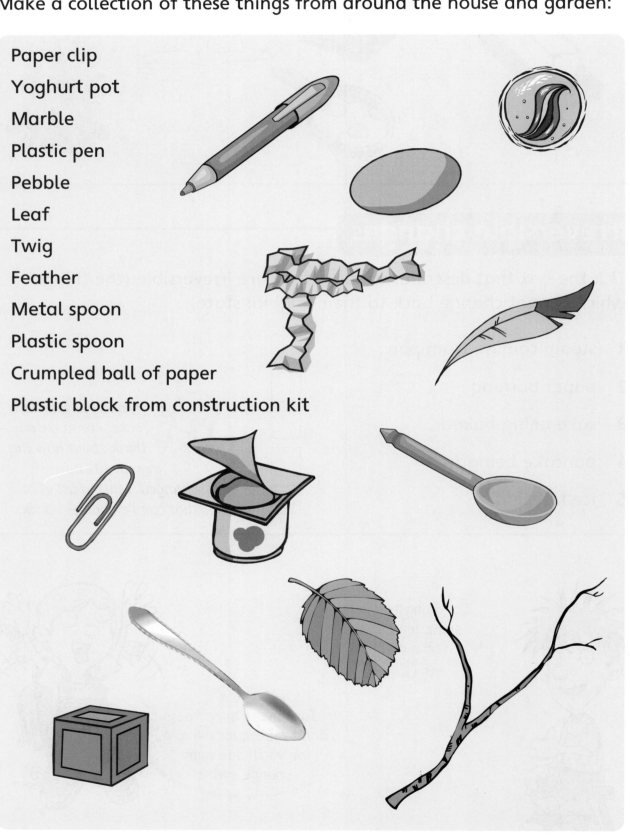

Testing objects

Fill a bowl (or your paddling pool!) with water. Fill in the table with your predictions of which things will float, and which will sink.

Then test the objects. Write 'float' or 'sink' in the results column.

object	my prediction	result
Paper clip		
Yoghurt pot		
Marble		
Plastic pen		
Pebble		
Leaf		
Twig		
Feather		
Metal spoon		
Plastic spoon		
Crumpled ball of paper		
Plastic block		

Were your predictions correct?

I'm off to play with my bath toys.

I'm going to sink my boat with some marbles!

Change investigation

Crispie cakes

Make some crispie cakes. Yes, it is cookery, but it also shows you how changes of state can be made. You will need an adult to help you, because this task involves handling things that are hot.

What you will need

You will need these things:

A block of chocolate

Crispie breakfast cereal

A bowl that can go in the microwave

A spoon

Cake cases

What to do

Break the chocolate into the bowl. Then melt it in the microwave. REVERSIBLE CHANGE ALERT! Chocolate has changed from a solid to a liquid.

Mix the crispie cereal into the liquid chocolate.

Spoon the mixture into the cake cases and leave in a cool place to set. REVERSIBLE CHANGE ALERT! Chocolate has changed from a liquid back to a solid.

You could try making chocolate-coated fruits too – grapes and strawberries are particularly yummy!

 Top Tip *You can add mini marshmallows or raisins to the mix to make the cakes extra-tasty!*

 I never realised science could be so tasty!

Yum!

Electricity

Which ones use electricity?

Draw a circle round the things that use electricity.

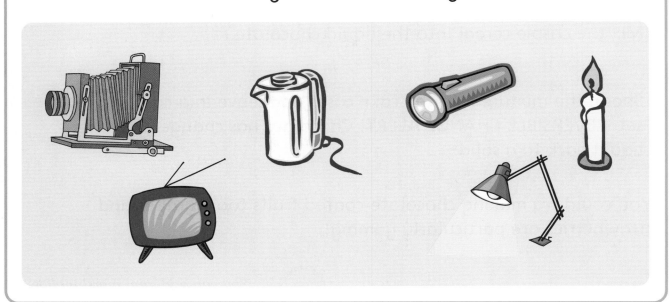

Battery or mains?

Battery or mains electricity? Tick the things that use electricity from a socket in the wall (mains electricity).

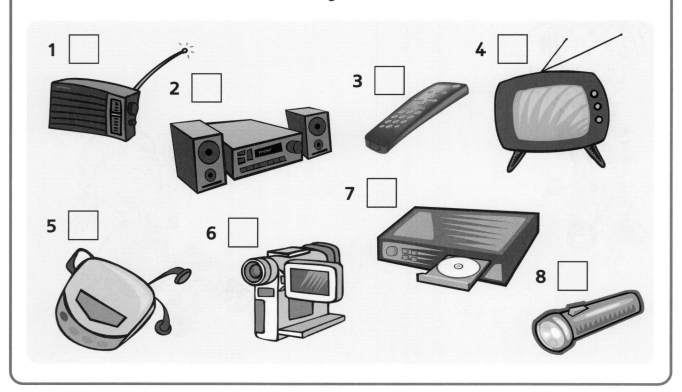

Sound sources

Draw a circle round the things that use electricity to make sound.

Match it up

Draw a line to match the beginning of each sentence to the second half, so they make sense.

1 Mains electricity

2 Electricity can be used to make heat, like

3 Torches use

4 Electricity can be used to make light,

5 Never poke anything in an electric socket

a ...lovely warm electric fires.

b ...electricity from batteries.

c ...is the type we get from sockets in the wall.

d ...because it can be very dangerous!

e ...like the light we get from lamps.

Top Tip *Never open or burn a battery. The chemicals inside can hurt you.*

Have you seen my torch?

No, I can't find it, because it's too dark...

Sound

Sounds good!

Look at these sentences. Tick the ones that are true.

1   Sound travels in invisible waves through the air. ☐

2   We can see sound waves. ☐

3   We hear things as sound enters our ears. ☐

4   We hear things as sound enters our noses. ☐

5   Things sound loudest the closer we are to the thing making the noise. ☐

6   Things sound loudest the further away we are from the thing making the noise. ☐

Safe sounds

Write down the answers to these questions.

1   Why should you never poke things in your ears?

_____

2   What noises might you hear in a town?

_____

3   What things make loud sounds? Write down four.

_____

4   What things make quiet sounds? Write down four.

_____

5   Why do people wear ear protectors when they are using loud machinery?

_____

Hear, hear

Circle the place you think the dog sounds loudest – area A, B, or C.

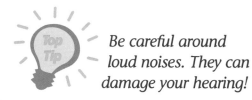

Be careful around loud noises. They can damage your hearing!

Loud or quiet?

Go on a sounds walk – in your home if you are alone, or outside if you are with a grown-up. Make a list of all the sounds you hear. Mark the loud sounds with 'L' and the quiet sounds with 'Q'.

_____

_____

_____

_____

_____

_____

_____

_____

I like LOUD noises!

Must be why you like me!

Forces

Push or pull?

Write 'push' or 'pull' in the boxes below each picture to describe the forces.

1 _____ 2 _____ 3 _____ 4 _____ 5 _____

Gravity

Complete these sentences about gravity by writing in the correct word from the box.

> force   smaller   fall   float   Moon   pulled

1 Gravity is a _____.

2 Gravity is the force that makes things _____ to the ground when you drop them.

3 Everything is _____ towards the centre of the Earth by gravity.

4 Without gravity, things would _____ about!

5 Gravity is not as strong on the _____ as on the Earth.

6 Gravity is not as strong on the Moon, because the Moon is much _____ than the Earth.

I wonder why mum says there's always friction when we're together?

It's because you're always rubbing me up the wrong way!

Friction

Which has more friction? Tick the correct box.

1 walking on ☐ wet tiles
    or ☐ dry tiles?

2 walking on ☐ an icy path
    or ☐ a dry path?

3 sledging on ☐ a snowy hill
    or ☐ a hill with no snow?

4 skidding on ☐ an icy playground
    or ☐ a dry playground?

5 rubbing together ☐ dry hands
    or ☐ wet hands

6 rubbing together ☐ wet hands
    or ☐ soapy wet hands?

Which force?

1 Which force stops us from slipping?

_____

2 Which force makes things fall when we drop them?

_____

3 Why are we more likely to slip on a wet floor than a dry floor?

_____

4 Which force makes our hands warm up when we rub them together on a cold day?

_____

5 Which makes more friction – a rough surface or a smooth surface?

_____

Top Tip *Have a go at rubbing your hands together:*
1. when they are dry
2. when they are wet
3. when they are wet and soapy.
How do they feel different to each other?

Sources of light

Things that give off light

Draw a circle round the things that are sources of light.

Lovely light

Look at these sentences. Tick the ones that are true.

1   Light travels in straight lines.

2   Light bends around objects that get in its way.

3   We see things when light bounces off them and into our eyes.

4   A fire is a source of light.

5   A candle is a source of light.

6   A torch is not a source of light.

7   A sequin is not a source of light, but it is shiny, because it reflects light.

Top Tip

Remember, shiny things are not sources of light. They just reflect it, like the Moon!

Let it glow!

Look at this picture of a bedroom. Now draw a circle round all of the sources of light you can see.

Can you see it?

Draw a beam of light to show how the cat can see the mouse.

I don't like the dark much, so I like sources of light.

Yes, but I like the dark. I can creep around and make you jump!

Shadows

Shadows

Draw a line to match the first and second parts of the sentences about shadows so they make sense!

1   Your shadow is made

2   Light travels in

3   Shadows are short and fat at midday

4   Shadows show us

5   Shadows are longest

a   ...when the Sun is high overhead.

b   ...straight lines.

c   ...in the late afternoon.

d   ...where the light has not been able to pass through an object.

e   ...because you block the light.

Shadow puppets

Can you explain how the boy is making the bird shadow on the screen?

_____

_____

_____

_____

_____

_____

_____

Changing shadows

Look at the shadow of this cat. Match the labels to the correct picture.

1

2

a The Sun is overhead, high in the sky, so the cat's shadow is short and fat.

b The Sun is low in the sky in the late afternoon, so the cat's shadow is tall and thin.

Where is the Sun?

Draw the Sun in three places: at sunrise, midday and sunset. Write the words as labels under each Sun you draw.

N

Top Tip *Check out how shadows move through the day. Chalk round a shadow at midday, and again at about 4pm. How have things changed?*

I like it when my shadow is tall and thin.

I like it when I jump on your shadow!

Light investigation

Make a simple sundial

You will need these things:

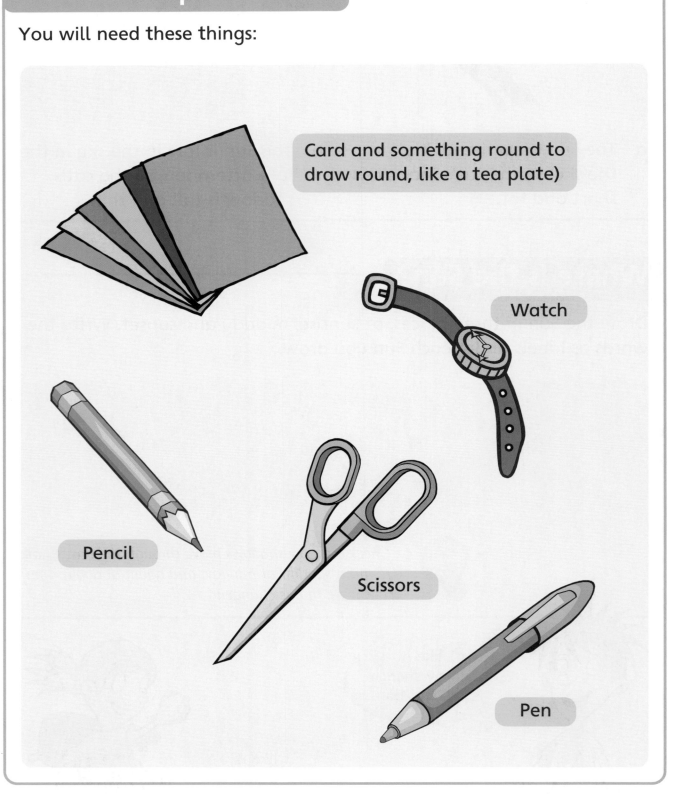

Card and something round to draw round, like a tea plate)

Watch

Pencil

Scissors

Pen

What to do

1   Draw around the tea plate onto your card.

2   Cut out the circle.

3   Push the pencil through the centre of your circle (you can find the centre by drawing lines that cross through the middle of the circle).

4   Stick the pencil in the ground, with the circle attached. It should be in a very sunny spot.

5   Mark the position of the shadow of the pencil on each hour (look at your watch). Draw a line and label it with the time.

The next day, you will not need a watch, because you have a sundial!

Top Tip *You can make a weatherproof sundial from plastic packaging and mark the hours in waterproof felt pen.*

Now we can even tell the time in the garden.

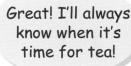

Great! I'll always know when it's time for tea!

Test practice

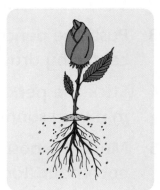

1 In the boxes below, draw a picture of the part of the plant above the description of the job it does.

a Attracts insects with its scent and colour.

b Holds the plant in the ground.

c Makes food using sunlight.

2 In the boxes below, draw the parts of the body we use for each sense.

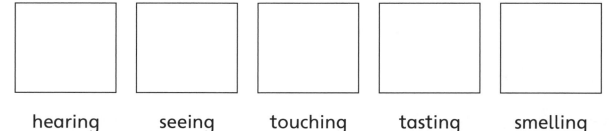

hearing   seeing   touching   tasting   smelling

3 List six pieces of rubbish that could be recycled.

a _____

b _____

c _____

d _____

e _____

f _____

4 Draw four things that are alive in the flower shape below.

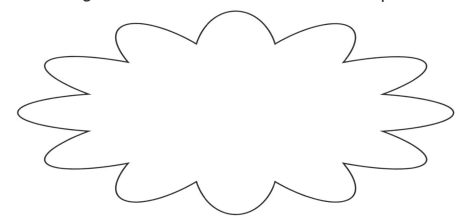

5 Sort these creatures into the two groups below.

robin   dog   penguin   butterfly   horse   crab

can fly

cannot fly

6 Tick the foods in each pair that are the healthier choices.

a apples ☐

or

apple pie ☐

c cheese pasties ☐

or

cubes of cheese ☐

b orange juice ☐

or

orange squash ☐

d milk ☐

or

cola ☐

7 Draw a line to match the bones to the part of the body they protect.

1 skull

2 pelvis

3 ribs

a heart and lungs

b brain

c bladder

8 Fill in the answers.

    a Write down the teeth that are used for grinding food.   _____

    b Write down the teeth that a dog uses for tearing meat.   _____

    c Write down the teeth that a rabbit uses for chopping carrots.   _____

9 Draw three natural objects in the basket shape.

10 List of six things that would sink in a bowl of water.

    a _____

    b _____

    c _____

    d _____

    e _____

    f _____

11 Choose the best material to make each object, then join them with a line.

1	metal	**a**	door
2	wood	**b**	lunchbox
3	glass	**c**	comic
4	plastic	**d**	window
5	paper	**e**	lorry

12 Solid, liquid or gas? Write 'S', 'L' or 'G' to explain the state of these things:

a metal ☐   **b** milk ☐   **c** apple ☐   **d** steam ☐

e orange juice ☐   **f** wood ☐   **g** air ☐   **h** petrol ☐

13 Tick the thing that can be changed back to the way it started.

a An egg that has been boiled. ☐

b A meringue that has been cooked. ☐

c Coal that has been burnt. ☐

d Ice that has melted. ☐

14 Tick the items that are a source of light.

a Moon ☐   **g** car headlight ☐   **l** window ☐

b fire ☐   **h** TV (turned on) ☐   **m** sequins ☐

c mirror ☐   **i** candle ☐   **n** computer monitor (turned on) ☐

d Sun ☐   **j** lamp ☐

e torch ☐   **k** glitter ☐

f aluminium foil ☐

15 Draw three things that use battery electricity.

16 Where do you think the radio sounds loudest? Mark the place with a circle.

17 a Write down the force that makes things fall to the ground when they are dropped.

_____

b Write down the force that stops us from slipping over.

_____

18 Explain below how the girl sees the butterfly.

_____

_____

19 Draw the shadow of a car at the following times:

a midday and the Sun is overhead, high in the sky.

b when the Sun is low in the sky in the late afternoon.